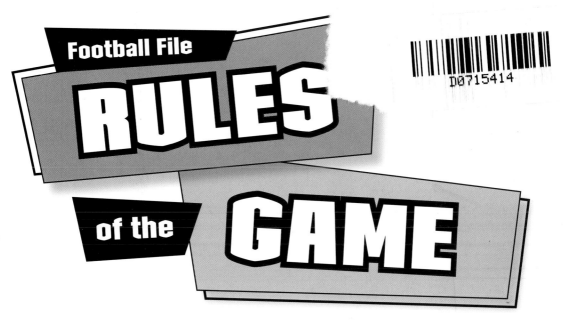

Football File

RULES

of the GAME

James Nixon

Photography by Bobby Humphrey

W

This edition 2014

Franklin Watts
338 Euston Road
London NW1 3BH

Franklin Watts Australia
Level 17/207 Kent Street
Sydney NSW 2000

© Franklin Watts 2010, 2014

ISBN 978 1 4451 3107 8

Dewey classification number:
796,3'3402022

A CIP catalogue record for this
publication is available from the
British Library.

Planning and production by
Discovery Books Limited
Editor: James Nixon
Design: Blink Media

The author, packager and publisher
would like to thank the children of
Farsley Celtic Junior Football Club for
their participation in this book.

Printed in China

Franklin Watts is a division
of Hachette Children's Books,
an Hachette UK Company.
www.hachette.co.uk

Photo acknowledgements:
Getty Images: pp. 5 top (Shaun Botterill), 8 (Alex Grimm/Bongarts), 11b (Bongarts), 13 bottom (Andrew Yates/AFP), 21 top (Frederick Breedon), 22 bottom (Daniel Garcia/AFP), 23 bottom (Vladimir Rys/Bongarts), 28 (Michael Steele)); Istockphoto.com: p. 14 top; Shutterstock: pp. 4 (Jonathan Larsen), 11t (EfecreataPhotography), 15 top (Shawn Pecor), 15 middle (Jonathan Larsen), 17b (photofriday), 19 top (Brandon Parry), 21 bottom (Andreas Gradin), 22 top (George Green), 25 bottom (Sport Graphic), 26 top (Adam Gasson), 26 left (Jonathan Larsen), 26 right (Sportsphotographer.eu), 27 left (Alvaro Alexander), 27 right (Sport Graphic), 27 bl (Matt Trommer), 29l Laszio Szirtesi), 29 bla (Maxisport); Wikimedia: p. 20 top.

Cover photos: Shutterstock: left (Sandro Donda), right (Trybex).

Every attempt has been made to clear copyright. Should there be any inadvertent omission please apply to the publisher for rectification.

Statistics on pages 28–29 are correct at the time of going to press, but in the fast-moving world of football are subject to change.

Contents

Words that appear in **bold** are in the glossary on page 30.

The LAWS of the game

To be a good footballer you need to understand the laws of the game. Knowing what is and is not allowed on a football pitch can give you an edge over your opponents in matches. On the other hand, not knowing the rules can be very costly for your team.

The basics

A football match is played between two teams with 11 players on each side. One player on each team is the goalkeeper. The aim is to score more goals than the opposition. Players have 90 minutes in which to score.

The match is split into two halves of 45 minutes. After the half-time break, the teams switch ends to shoot the other way. The referee can add on time at the end of each half, if time has been lost for injuries, **substitutions** and other stoppages.

The rulebook

Compared to other sports, football is a very simple game. The rulebook has just 17 sections of law. For example, this is Law 10 (right):

Law 10 – The Method of Scoring

'A goal is scored when the whole of the ball passes over the goal line, between the goalposts and under the crossbar,...The team scoring the greater number of goals in the match is the winner.'

EXPERT: Mats Hummels

Defenders must do everything they can to stop attackers scoring a goal. But, they must defend within the laws of the game. If they break the rules they can give away dangerous **free kicks** or even a **penalty** to their opponents. This gives the opposition a great chance to score. German star Mats Hummels (far right) is skilful at defending without giving away fouls. His strength, determination and tackling skills win him the ball. To avoid tripping players, the timing of his tackles is usually spot-on.

The FIELD of PLAY

The field of play is where all the action takes place. White lines mark the boundary and other parts of the pitch. A football pitch must be rectangular in shape, but the overall size of a pitch can vary.

Pitch size

A pitch can be between 100 to 130 yards (90-120 metres) long and 50 to 100 yards (45-90 m) wide. Even in the professional game pitch sizes can be very different. The field of play inside Real Madrid's Bernabeu stadium is 6 m longer and 4 m wider than the pitch at Liverpool's Anfield ground!

50 to 100 yards (45-90 m)

100 to 130 yards (90-120 m)

1. **Halfway line** – divides the field of play into two equal halves.
2. **Centre spot** – where the match kicks off or restarts.
3. **Centre circle** – This marks a distance of 10 yards (9.15 m) from the centre spot. At kick-offs you cannot enter this circle until the opponents kick-off.
4. **Penalty area** – The only part of the pitch where the goalkeeper can handle the ball. This area is sometimes called 'the box'.
5. **Penalty spot** – A foul in your own penalty area usually means a penalty to your opponents. The penalty kick is taken from this spot, 12 yards (11 m) from goal.
6. **The 'D'** – marks a distance of 10 yards (9.15 m) away from the penalty spot.
7. **Six-yard box** – marks where goalkeepers take their goal kicks.
8. **Touchlines** – A ball that crosses the touchlines (or sidelines) is out of play. Play restarts from a throw-in.
9. **Goal lines** – A ball that completely crosses this line either side of the goal, results in a goal kick or a corner being awarded.
10. **Corner quadrants** – Corner kicks must be taken from on or inside this arc.
11. **Goals**

Goalposts

The goals are located on the centre of each goal line. They are 8 yards (7.32 m) wide and 8 feet (2.4 m) high. The goalposts and crossbar must be painted white.

Starts and restarts

To start a match or half, or restart after a goal, play begins from the centre spot. At the kick-off, all players must be in their own half. The kicker must play the ball forward and cannot touch it again until it has touched another player. You could actually run up and shoot at goal straight from the kick-off!

Centre circle

The EQUIPMENT

Footballers by law must wear a shirt, shorts, socks, shinpads and football boots. The goalkeeper will also wear gloves. The kit might seem basic, but players must choose the correct type of kit and look after their equipment if they want to play to their full potential.

Boots

The most important thing is to find a pair of boots that fit well. Football boots should fit snugly to your foot and support your ankle. But you shouldn't squeeze your foot into a size too small. A good boot is made of soft leather so you can feel the football. It should also be flexible to help the movement of your foot.

Moulds or screw-ins

Boots can either have moulded studs or screw-in studs. **Moulds** (left) give you better support on dry pitches. If you wear screw-ins (above) on a hard pitch you will probably get blisters. Screw-in studs are better on muddy ground as they give you more grip. If you buy just one pair of boots buy a screw-in pair, which can be fitted with different lengths of studs for various surfaces.

Safety rules

Players must not wear anything that is dangerous to themselves or others. The rules ban certain sizes and shapes of studs. The referee will check each player's studs before a game. You must also take off any kind of jewellery. Shinpads must be worn at all levels of the game. They are made out of a light but strong plastic and they protect your lower leg from serious injury. There are different types, so find out which is best for you.

These shinpads have padding around the ankle bone for extra protection.

Boot care

Nobody likes cleaning their boots after the game. But, if you don't they can crack and go hard, and your game will suffer. Always knock off the mud after a match and clean the rest with a damp cloth. Let them dry naturally – do not put them by a heater! Stuff your boots with newspaper, so they hold their shape when you are not wearing them.

Colour clashes

The two teams must wear different-coloured shirts. That is why football clubs have home and away strips. The away team will use their second strip if their normal kit clashes with the opposition's. The goalkeeper's clothing must also be a different colour to the outfield players and referee.

The REFEREE

A football match cannot be played without a referee. With the help of two assistants on the touchline, it is their job to control the game.

The referee makes sure that all the players stick to the rules. They blow a whistle and use hand signals to communicate their decisions to players. The referee's decision is final!

Respect the ref

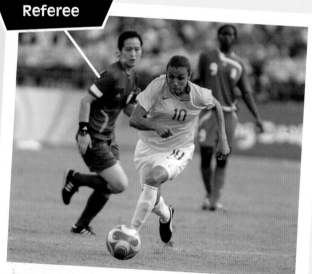

Referee

Refereeing is a very tough job. Football is a fast-moving game, played on a big pitch. Referees have to be extremely fit to keep up with the play. They do more running in a match than any of the players! Decisions have to be made in a split-second. They don't get to see a slow-motion television replay from five different angles! A referee is bound to get the odd decision wrong. If this happens, accept it. Never argue with the referee, or you will be **booked**.

Timekeeping

The referee doesn't just make judgements on fouls and whether the ball was in or out of play. They are also the timekeeper. They keep an eye on their watch and stop it for injuries and other stoppages. The end of the match is signalled with a long blow of the whistle.

EXPERT: Howard Webb

Englishman Howard Webb is considered to be one of the best referees in the world. More often than not he makes the right call. Webb was selected to referee the 2010 World Cup Final between Spain and the Netherlands. He communicates his decisions to players from around the globe by using clear and strong body language. By doing this, the players accept Webb's decisions and he gains their respect.

Whistle

Watch

Playing advantage

When the referee spots a foul, they can choose to let the game continue. They will do this if they feel the team would rather carry on playing than receive a free kick. To signal that the referee is 'playing advantage' they will extend both arms out in front of their body (right). Playing advantage helps to keep the game flowing. So, remember to play to the whistle – do not stop until you hear it.

Advantage

11

FOULS

If you break the law you can expect the referee to punish you. Depending on where your foul took place you will concede a free kick or a penalty. There are many types of foul you can give away, from shirt-pulling or tripping to handling the ball or time-wasting.

Shirt-pulling

Fouling opponents

When you challenge your opponent for the ball it must be done fairly. If you kick, trip, push or hold your opponent the referee will blow his whistle for a foul. You must make contact with the ball before the player as you tackle. It is no good saying you got the ball if you tackled your opponent first.

Trip

Dangerous play

A foul can also be awarded if the referee feels your challenge was dangerous. Tackling with your studs raised in the air (right) or **slide tackling** a player from behind will always be penalised. A two-footed challenge is also against the law. Be warned: if you play dangerously the referee may take matters further and send you off (see pages 14-15)!

Obstruction

A **shoulder barge**, where your arm is straight and you lean into the opponent is a legal challenge. However, it must be within playing distance of the ball. If you **obstruct** a player off the ball this is a foul.

You cannot impede the progress of a player if you are not within playing distance of the ball.

Handball

Players must not handle the ball with their hand or any part of their arm (above). If you handball deliberately you will concede a foul. It is often tough for a referee to decide whether the handball was deliberate or not. If you are a defender blocking a shot, the safest thing to do is to keep your hands down by your side.

Goalkeeper fouls

Goalkeepers can give away free kicks and penalties, too. There are extra rules for goalkeepers. Goalkeepers must be familiar with them. They cannot:

▸ hold on to the ball for longer than six seconds
▸ touch the ball with their hands straight after releasing it
▸ touch a back pass (played with the feet) or a throw-in from a teammate with their hands
▸ handle the ball outside their own penalty area.

CARD offences

Some fouls and offences are so serious that the referee will hand out extra punishment. A yellow card 'cautions' a player about their behaviour. If the referee shows a red card you are sent off the field and your match is over!

A player who is red carded has really let the other players down. The team have to play the rest of the match with only ten players (or less if someone else has already been sent off).

Bookings

A yellow card is also known as a 'booking'. This is because the referee takes your name and shirt number, and makes a note of the yellow card in their notebook. If you receive two yellow cards in a match it means a red card and you are sent off.

The offences below will see the ref reaching for the yellow card:

- a bad, reckless or deliberate foul
- persistent fouling (the referee may speak to you and give a verbal warning before showing yellow)
- time-wasting, such as delaying the restart of play
- failing to retreat 10 yards (9.15 m) from a free kick or corner
- diving
- arguing with the referee, known as **dissent**
- professionals can be booked for over-the-top goal celebrations, such as removing their shirt, jumping into the crowd or pulling out the corner flag!

Gentleman Jim

Between 1946 and 1965 defender Jimmy Dickinson played 893 games for England and Portsmouth, and incredibly did not get booked once! He earned himself the nickname 'Gentleman Jim'.

Bans and fines

Getting booked or sent off doesn't just land you in trouble on the pitch. At all levels of the game, players will receive a fine for being carded. If you get a red card you will also get a **suspension**. This means you are banned from playing for a certain number of matches.

Seeing red

For the most extreme offences you will be shown a straight red card. There is no excuse for being sent off. Your teammates, your supporters and your manager will be furious with you.

Handball

Red-card offences include:

▶ a dangerous tackle (e.g. two-footed, high)
▶ violent conduct, such as punching and kicking (never raise your hands to an opponent or the referee)
▶ spitting at an opponent
▶ using insulting language or **gestures**
▶ fouling to prevent a clear goalscoring opportunity (e.g. handling the ball on your goal line (left) or tripping an attacker who is through on goal).

15

OFFSIDE

The offside law, designed to stop forwards **goal-hanging**, is probably the most difficult law to understand. It is also a law that causes much debate and controversy.

The referee must judge if the player in an offside position is interfering with play. There is a difference between being in an offside position and committing an offside offence.

Offside position

It is not an offence to be in an offside position. But, you will be flagged offside if a teammate passes to you.

▸ You are in an offside position if you are ahead of every opponent on the pitch except one (usually the goalkeeper).

▸ To be in an onside position you need two opponents (including goalkeeper) between you and the goal.

▸ If you are level with the last defender you are onside. You can be caught offside if any part of your body except your arms is ahead of the defender.

Here, any attacker between the black dotted line and the goal is in an offside position. (To be onside you need two opponents between you and the goal.)

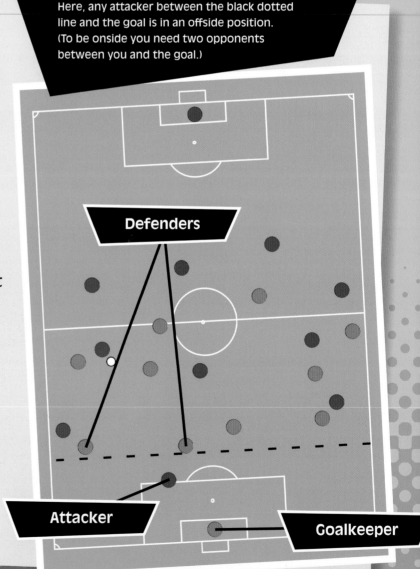

Defenders

Attacker

Goalkeeper

Offside flag

The flag will be raised by the assistant referee if you are in an offside position the exact moment the ball was passed to you (1). Even if the ball is not passed directly to you, you can still be offside. You will be flagged offside if you are interfering with play, or gaining an advantage by being in an offside position. Interfering with play can be standing in the goalkeeper's line of vision (2), or distracting a defender. You are gaining an advantage if a shot or pass finds its way to you via a **deflection**, such as a rebound off the keeper (3).

1

2

3

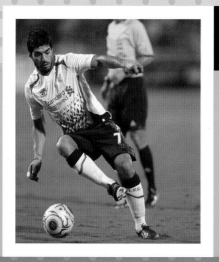

Not offside

You cannot be offside:
▸ if your teammate's pass to you was sideways or backwards
▸ from a throw-in or goal kick
▸ in your own half
▸ if you do not interfere with play.

EXPERT: Luis Suarez

Forwards have to be cunning if they want to break through a defence without being offside. Luis Suarez, Uruguay's all-time top goalscorer, is an expert at this. To stay onside, he delays his run until the second the pass is played. His pace then takes him away from the defenders. This helped him score 49 goals in just one season when he was at Ajax.

ASSISTANT referees

It would be impossible for a referee to run a match all by themselves. They would need eyes in the back of their head! The referee has two assistants to help them make decisions. One assistant (left) patrols each touchline. In the past, assistant referees were called linesmen or lineswomen.

Signals

The assistant grabs the referee's attention by waving a brightly coloured flag. The signal they make tells the referee their decision.

This assistant is signalling a throw-in to the team attacking the goal to his left.

Duties

The assistant referee's duties are:
▸ to indicate the ball out of play for a throw-in, goal, corner or goal kick
▸ to decide which team has touched the ball out of play
▸ to flag for fouls that happen near to them
▸ to judge offside decisions. The referee relies on the assistant to make offside calls because they have the perfect view across the pitch. But, it is still not easy to get the decision right. They have to somehow keep an eye on the ball as it is kicked and the attacker at the same time.

Respect the assistants and do not argue with their decisions.

This assistant has raised her flag to indicate an offside in the middle of the pitch. She would point the flag down if the offside took place on her side of the pitch, and point it up if the offside was on the far side of the pitch.

Final say

The assistant referee can alert the referee to a foul that they have not spotted. But, the referee has the final say! They can overturn any decision the assistant makes, if they wish.

It is not always easy for an assistant to judge if the ball has crossed the line for a goal.

Goal-line technology

Assistant referees also have the tricky job of trying to spot if the ball has crossed the goal line for a goal. The whole of the ball has to cross the line. As they are standing at the side of the pitch this is not always easy to see, especially if players are blocking their view. In 2013 the English Premier League started using a computer system called Hawk-eye during its matches. The system uses seven cameras on each goal to analyse whether or not the ball has crossed the line. Stranger pieces of goal-line technology are also being developed. One idea is to use a microchip built into the football. When the ball crosses the line the microchip would send a bleeping signal into the earpiece of the referee. This would tell him or her that a goal has been scored.

Fourth official

At professional games there is now a fourth official to help the referee. They signal to a referee when a team wants to make a substitution. They do this with an electronic board. The board is also used to show the crowd and players how much **stoppage time** the referee has added on.

OUT of PLAY

When the whole of the ball crosses the outside lines of the pitch the ball is out of play and play needs to be restarted. Even if the ball curves over the line and back on to the pitch again, the ball is out of play. A goal kick, corner or throw-in will be awarded depending on where the ball went out and who last touched it.

Throw-in

If the ball crosses the sidelines, a throw-in is given to the team who did not touch the ball out. This is taken from where the ball crossed the line. Here is how you should throw-in:

▸ Using both hands, spread your fingers behind the ball so your thumbs are nearly touching (1).
▸ Bring the ball forwards from behind and over your head (2).
▸ Keep a part of both feet on the ground, on or behind the touchline.
▸ Follow through with your hands and fingers to direct the flight of the ball (3).

Foul throws

You must throw-in correctly. If you don't, the referee will award a throw-in to the other side. Foul throws include lifting a foot off the floor, stepping over the sideline and not bringing the ball back behind your head (right). You cannot score from a throw-in and the goalkeeper cannot handle a throw from a teammate.

EXPERT: Kelley O'Hara

Most teams have a throw-in expert, who can launch long, accurate throws. Kelley O'Hara does this job for the women's USA team. She takes a couple of quick paces towards the sideline, and with a leading leg in front of the other, she arches her back right back and thrusts forward. A long throw is a very useful weapon. It can cause havoc in the opposition's penalty box.

Goal kick

When the attackers knock the ball over the goal line, to the sides of the goal, the defence is awarded a goal kick. The goal kick can be taken by any player from any point inside the six-yard box (right). But, the kick must leave the penalty area before any player can touch it.

Corner

If the defenders knock the ball across their own goal line (to the sides of the goal) it is a corner kick. This is taken in the quadrant from the side of the pitch the ball left the field. Once the kick is taken another player must touch it, before the kicker can touch it again. If the corner-taker touches it twice, the opposition receives an indirect free kick (see pages 22-23).

FREE KICKS

There are two types of free kick depending on the type of foul. They can be direct or indirect. A direct free kick can be shot straight into the net. An indirect free kick has to touch another player before a goal can be scored. Try to avoid giving away free kicks around the penalty area. They give the opposition a chance to shoot at goal or cross into the box.

Stand back

A free kick is taken from the place where the foul was committed. The defending side must retreat and stand 10 yards (9.15 m) away from the free kick. You cannot move forward to block the free kick until the ball is struck. If you do, the referee will order a retake and you will be booked! As on a corner, the kicker can only touch it once, before it touches another player.

Ref's signals

The referee points forward with a raised arm to show the direction in which a direct free kick is awarded.

To indicate an indirect free kick the referee raises his hand right above his head.

10 yards

Direct or indirect

Most offences, such as tripping or handball, result in a direct free kick. Indirect free kicks are awarded for:

▸ blocking an opponent not within playing distance of the ball

▸ dangerous play, such as a challenge with a high foot

▸ taking two touches when taking a corner, throw-in, free kick or kick-off

▸ the goalkeeper handling a back pass.

Goalmouth scramble

Indirect free kicks inside the opposition's penalty area can be bizarre. The defenders will often cram themselves on the goal line between the posts. As an attacker you can shoot on goal and hope for a deflection on the way, or you can tap it sideways for a teammate to shoot (below). But beware: the mass of defenders will charge at you as soon as the free kick is taken, so you have to be quick.

No goal

If you score direct from an indirect free kick it will not count! Instead the opposition will be awarded a goal kick.

PENALTIES

To give away a penalty is one of the worst mistakes you can make as a footballer. For the opposition it is the perfect chance to score. A penalty kick can be the difference between winning and losing a match. A foul that would normally be a direct free kick is a penalty if it happens inside your penalty box.

Paying the penalty

What makes a penalty such a good chance to score? For a start, the kick is taken from a spot, which is only 12 yards (11 m) away from goal. The penalty-taker has just the goalkeeper to beat (right). No other player can interfere until the ball has been struck. The keeper has to stay on their line until the ball is kicked. If they move off their line too soon to save it, the kick will be retaken.

Keep out!

All the other players on the field must stay behind the penalty spot, and keep out of the penalty box and 'D' until the kick is taken. You should be on your toes and rush in when the penalty is struck. There may be the chance of a rebound. But, the referee can order a retake if any player enters the area too soon.

Rebounds

Once the penalty is taken the kicker cannot touch it again until it has touched another player. So, if your penalty rebounds off the post or crossbar, leave it alone. But, be ready for a rebound off the keeper. You may get a second chance to put it in the net.

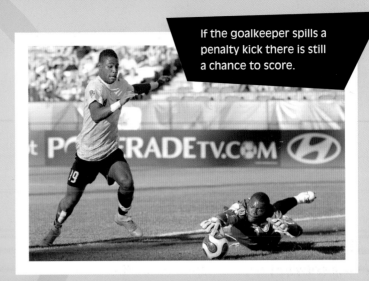

If the goalkeeper spills a penalty kick there is still a chance to score.

The keeper's view

The chances of you saving a penalty are small. But if you do pull it off you will be a hero. You can't move off your line before the ball is kicked, but you can move along it. Some keepers bounce up and down in an attempt to put the striker off. It is not possible to react in time to a well-placed shot into the corner. However, you can try to guess which way the ball will go (above). Try to watch the taker carefully and dive just before the kick is struck. As you dive sideways, stretch out and spread yourself big.

Shoot-outs

Unlike a league game, a **cup tie** cannot be drawn. If a replay and **extra time** cannot produce a winner, the game will be decided by a dramatic penalty shoot-out. Five players on each side take a penalty. If the scores are still level, it is then **sudden death**! An extra player from each team steps up, and this continues until there is a winner.

FAIR play

Alongside the rules of the game, the world football organisation (FIFA) has a 'code of conduct'. This is a list of ways in which footballers should behave on and off the field. The code is known as the Fair Play Programme. Each rule is based around respect: for the rules, officials and opponents.

Before each professional game players shake hands with the officials and the opposition.

The code

▶ Observe the laws of the game.
▶ Do not cheat. Pretending to be fouled is unacceptable. You will be booked.
▶ Play fair. If the ball is kicked out of play by your opponents because a player is badly injured, make sure you return the ball to them from the restart.
▶ Play to win, but accept defeat properly. Shake hands with the referee and opposition at the end of the game (right).
▶ Respect everyone involved in the game. Do not show violence or aggression to opponents or referees. Remember: the referee's decision is final!

Banned!

Not playing in the spirit of the game can land a professional player in trouble. A dive to con the referee or a stamp on a player's leg may go unnoticed on the pitch. However, the television cameras see everything. The player can expect to be banned and fined for their actions. A match-ban can last many months if the offence is serious.

Diving is cheating. Do not do it – you will be booked and could receive a match ban, too.

Respect campaign

The English Football Association (FA) has launched a campaign to make sure referees are treated properly. This is aimed at footballers at all levels of the game. On average, 7,000 referees are quitting football every year, because of the abuse they receive from players and spectators. Do not confront and **harass** the referee – accept their decisions. Without referees there would be no football matches, so give the ref respect.

Fair Play Award

The Fair Play Award is occasionally given to players or teams. Italian striker Paulo Di Canio (right) was a past winner of the award for his special moment of **sportsmanship**. He could have scored past an injured goalkeeper lying on the ground. Instead he picked up the ball and stopped the game!

The MANAGERS

The head of a football team is known as the manager. More pressure falls on their shoulders than any other person at the club. If results are going badly, it is the manager who gets the blame. The importance of a good manager, who can motivate the players and choose the correct team and **tactics** is huge. A manager will try to use the rules of the game to their team's advantage.

Manager David Moyes gives instructions to Wayne Rooney who is about to be substituted into a game in an attempt to swing the match in their team's favour.

On the training ground

During the week the manager will prepare their team for the next game. They will work on specific tactics. For example, they may work with the defence on playing an **offside trap**. They will also instruct the players on how they should defend set pieces, such as corners and free kicks.

Substitutes

Once the team talk is over and the match has kicked off, it is out of the manager's hands – or is it? The manager can influence a game by making substitutions, or changing tactics or formation. In most competitions the rules allow up to three substitutions in a match. The substitution can only be made once the referee is ready. A substitute with fresh legs can have a big impact on a match. Once a player is substituted they cannot be used again.

Top managers

Jose Mourinho

Nation: Portugal   **D.O.B:** 26.01.63

CLUB RECORD

TEAM	FROM	TO	G	W	D	L	WIN %
BENFICA	20 SEPTEMBER 2000	5 DECEMBER 2000	11	6	3	2	54.55
LEIRIA	14 APRIL 2001	20 JANUARY 2002	29	15	8	6	51.72
PORTO	23 JANUARY 2002	26 MAY 2004	124	90	21	13	72.58
CHELSEA	2 JUNE 2004	20 SEPTEMBER 2007	185	124	40	21	67.03
INTER MILAN	2 JUNE 2008	28 MAY 2010	108	67	26	15	62.04
REAL MADRID	31 MAY 2010	1 JUNE 2013	178	128	28	22	71.91
CHELSEA	2 JUNE 2008	PRESENT	4	2	2	0	50.00

Honours: Portuguese League 2003, 2004; Portuguese Cup 2003; UEFA Cup 2003; Champions League 2004, 2010; Premier League 2005, 2006; FA Cup 2007; Italian League 2009, 2010; Italian Cup 2010; Spanish Cup 2011, Spanish League 2012

André Villas-Boas

Nation: Portugal   **D.O.B:** 17.10.77

CLUB RECORD

TEAM	FROM	TO	G	W	D	L	WIN %
ACADÉMICA	14 OCTOBER 2009	2 JUNE 2010	30	11	9	10	36.67
PORTO	2 JUNE 2010	21 JUNE 2011	58	49	5	4	84.48
CHELSEA	22 JUNE 2011	4 MARCH 2012	40	19	11	10	47.50
TOTTENHAM HOTSPUR	3 JULY 2012	PRESENT	59	31	16	12	52.54

Honours: Portuguese League 2011; Portuguese Cup 2011; UEFA Europa League 2011

Arsene Wenger

Nation: France   **D.O.B:** 22.10.49

CLUB RECORD

TEAM	FROM	TO	G	W	D	L	WIN %
NANCY	1 JULY 1984	1 JULY 1987	114	33	30	51	28.95
MONACO	1 JULY 1987	17 SEPTEMBER 1994	266	130	53	83	48.87
NAGOYA GRAMPUS	9 DECEMBER 1994	30 SEPTEMBER 996	56	38	0	18	67.86
ARSENAL	30 SEPTEMBER 1996	PRESENT	959	547	228	148	57.00

Honours: French League 1979; French Cup 1991; Japanese Cup 1996; Japanese League 1996; Premier League 1998, 2002, 2004; FA Cup 1998, 2002, 2003, 2005

Carlo Ancelotti

Nation: Italy   **D.O.B:** 10.06.59

CLUB RECORD

TEAM	FROM	TO	G	W	D	L	WIN %
REGGIANA	11 AUGUST 1995	31 MAY 1996	41	17	14	10	41.46
PARMA	1 AUGUST 1996	31 MAY 1998	87	42	27	18	48.28
JUVENTUS	9 FEBRUARY 1999	31 MAY 2001	114	63	33	18	55.26
AC MILAN	6 NOVEMBER 2001	31 MAY 2009	423	238	101	84	56.26
CHELSEA	1 JULY 2009	22 MAY 2011	109	67	20	22	61.47
PARIS SAINT-GERMAIN	30 DECEMBER 2011	25 June 2013	77	49	19	9	63.64
REAL MADRID	25 JUNE 2013	PRESENT	3	3	0	0	100.00

Honours: Italian Cup 2003; Italian League 2004; Champions League 2003, 2007; Premier League 2010; FA Cup 2010, French League 2013

Pep Guardiola

Nation: Scotland   **D.O.B:** 31.12.41

CLUB RECORD

TEAM	FROM	TO	G	W	D	L	WIN %
BARCELONA	1 JULY 2008	30 JUNE 2012	247	179	47	21	72.47
BAYERN MUNICH	26 JUNE 2013	PRESENT	7	4	2	1	57.14

Honours: Honours: Spanish League 2009, 2010, 2011; Spanish Cup 2009, 2012; Champions League 2009, 2011; FIFA Club World Cup 2009, 2011

Silvia Neid

Nation: Germany   **D.O.B:** 2.05.64

CLUB RECORD

TEAM	FROM	TO	G	W	D	L	WIN %
GERMANY	20 JUNE 2005	PRESENT	121	87	18	16	71.90

Honours: World Cup 2007; European Championships 2009, 2013

Statistics in this book are correct at the time of going to press, but in the fast-moving world of football are subject to change.

Glossary

booked shown a yellow card by the referee. Two yellow cards in a game and you will be sent off.

cup tie a match in a competition where teams get knocked out until there is one winner

deflection when the ball hits a player and veers off in a different direction

dissent arguing with the referee

extra time an extra 30 minutes added to a drawn match, split into two halves each lasting 15 minutes

foul an action which breaks the rules of the game, such as tripping, pushing, handball, etc

free kick a kick of the ball awarded to a side because of a foul by the opposition

gesture a movement with the body or hands to express your feelings

goal-hanging spending most of your time near the opponent's goal in the hope of scoring easy goals

harass behave aggressively towards someone

indirect free kick a free kick (awarded for certain fouls) that cannot be struck directly into the goal

moulds plastic studs which are moulded to the sole of a football boot and cannot be removed

obstruct deliberately block a player's movement with your body

offside a position on the field where the ball cannot be passed to you. To be onside you must have two opponents between you and the opponent's goal.

offside trap a tactic that a team's defence uses to catch an opponent offside

penalty a shot from the penalty spot (11 metres from goal) with just the goalkeeper to beat. It is awarded to the opposition when the defending side have fouled in their own penalty area.

shoulder barge a lean of the body into your opponent to legally push them off the ball

slide tackling sliding the body feet-forward to take the ball from the player in possession

sportsmanship showing fair play to your opponents

stoppage time time added on to the end of each half of a football match for time lost due to injuries and substitutions

substitution when a player is taken off the field by the manager and replaced by someone else

sudden death where a penalty shoot-out continues until one side misses and the other scores, to decide the game

suspension a player with a suspension is prevented from playing for a certain period of time

tactics the plans and ideas used by a team to gain an edge over the opposition

Further information

Books

Rules of the Game (Football Focus), Clive Gifford, Wayland, 2012

Soccer (Know the Game), A & C Black, 2006

Soccer: The Ultimate Guide, DK Publishing, 2010

Websites

http://www.thefa.com/football-rules-governance
Home of the Football Association with links to the game's official rulebook.

http://news.bbc.co.uk/sport1/hi/football/rules_and_equipment/default.stm
This site includes a guide to equipment, officials and fouls, and has an in-depth explanation of the offside law.

www.talkfootball.co.uk/guides/rules_of_football.html
A guide to the rules of the game.

www.thefa.com/leagues/respect
Download the Respect campaign here.

Note to parents and teachers: Every effort has been made by the Publishers to ensure that these websites are suitable for children, that they are of the highest educational value, and that they contain no inappropriate or offensive material. However, because of the nature of the Internet, it is impossible to guarantee that the contents of these sites will not be altered. We strongly advise that Internet access is supervised by a responsible adult.

DVDs

The History of Football. Fremantle Home Entertainment, 2004

Soccer Drills, Go Entertain, 2007

Index